Master Weaver from Ghana

Gilbert "Bobbo" Ahiagble
& Louise Meyer

Photographs by
Nestor Hernandez

OPEN HAND PUBLISHING, LLC
Greensboro, North Carolina

Sea mist and the salty smell of the Atlantic Ocean are part of everyday life in **Denu** (Deh-noo), a village in **Ghana** (Gah-nah) on the south coast of West Africa.

From his family's compound, Kweku (Kweh-koo) hears the waves as they break on the beach, and sees fish nets being cast out and drawn in again full of gleaming fish.

Kweku thinks all men are either weavers or fishermen. All the men in his family are weavers. His neighbors are fishermen.

In a way, fishermen are weavers too. They make and mend their nets, and help link the people of the coast together through trade. For centuries, fishermen have taken cloth with them in their boats as they travel from the mouth of the **Volta River** all the way to **Nigeria**.

Knowledge is passed on from father to son.

Gilbert "Bobbo" Ahiagble, (Bo-bo Ah-hee-ahg-blay) the master weaver, is Kweku's father. Bobbo, his wife Cecilia, and their extended family live in a large walled area called a compound. Inside are two houses and sandy courtyards shaded by mango and palm trees. The younger children live in one house with Bobbo and Cecilia. The older sisters and brothers live with their grandmother in the other house.

There is nothing more important than the family. They live and work together. They rely on one another. Their lives are woven together like threads on the loom.

Their lives are woven together like threads on the loom.

Every four days an open air market is held in Denu. Cecilia buys fresh, ripe fruit and vegetables for her family. Corn, peanuts, okra, onions, tomatoes, starchy cassava root, yams, and peppers are plentiful. The women walk home with their purchases gracefully balanced on their heads.

Kweku loves the delicious meals his mother prepares with the fresh ingredients she's purchased at the market. He especially likes fish. Fresh, salted, smoked, or sun-dried fish are served almost every day.

The women take turns carrying the new baby on their backs

5

Bobbo heads the family's weaving business. Kweku is too young to weave, but he has been paying attention. He already knows how to wash threads and wind thread on **bobbins.**

Brothers Grandi and Caphuchi weave after school and during school vacations. Big brothers Cliff and Kwame are weavers. Uncles Kobla, Yao and Kwajo weave, too.

Like fitness training, weaving requires energy, concentration, and skill. The elders say weaving keeps them smart, strong, happy, and healthy.

One thread is weak. Threads woven together are strong!

Uncles Kobla, Yao, and Kwajo work together in the shade.

Weaving together from sunrise to sunset has been the family's tradition for hundreds of years. The family is proud to keep the tradition alive.

Sons learn to weave by watching and helping their elders. Bobbo himself learned by observing and assisting his father in their native village of **Agbozume**, a few miles north of Denu. People come to the busy textile market in Agbozume to buy and sell the vibrant, highly prized **strip weaving.**

Yao examines a strip of weaving.

The people who live in this part of Africa are of the **Ewe** (Ay-vay) culture. They speak the Ewe language. It is believed that they migrated west from **Nigeria** about 500 years ago.

Ewe are hard-working, creative people. For centuries, weaving has been the men's primary art and occupation. There are excellent Ewe drummers and dancers, woodworkers and basket-makers, too. Most people also grow food. At planting time and harvest time, the weavers stop weaving to tend gardens or fields.

Many women have stalls in the market or near their homes, where they sell handcrafts, food, thread, or cloth. Often, it is the women in the family who manage the money.

Kweku's Aunt Awuye sells thread and dyes at the market.

To the west live the **Asante** (Ah-shan-tay) people. The majority of **Ghanaians** are Asante. They are known for their brilliantly colored **kente cloth**. Although Ewe strip weaving and Asante strip weaving are different, both are popularly called kente cloth.

For more than a thousand years, African textiles and treasures have been traded with people to the North. Cloth is traded as far away as Asia and the Mediterranean. Fine examples of strip weaving can be seen in museums and galleries around the world, including the Smithsonian African Art Museum in Washington, D.C.

Agbenyega Adedze

Colorful strip-woven cloth is sold in this market stall in Agbozume.

9

Ewe strip woven wrappers are worn for special occasions.

Richly patterned Ewe cloth is made from colorful, fine cotton, silk, or rayon thread. The thread is woven into long narrow strips. The strips are cut into even lengths and carefully sewn together to make a large piece of fabric called a **wrapper**. Traditionally, the wrapper is never cut. Men wear it draped over the left shoulder. Women wrap it around the hips to make a skirt, or around the upper body to make a baby carrier.

Once made only for royalty and rich people, today many people enjoy wearing it for very special occasions.

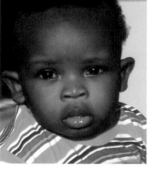

Cecilia is putting on her new wrapper. Bobbo wove it for her in honor of the birth of the newest weaver in the family. This is the most beautiful pattern the Ewe know how to weave. It is called **"worgagba,"** which means "corn power." Corn is their most important daily food.

All Ewe patterns have names and tell stories. Each color and design woven into the cloth has its own meaning. Memories recorded in the patterns are shared from generation to generation. Old cloth is especially valuable.

The pattern of Bobbo's big green wrapper is called **"sedavor,"** which means "fences make good friends." It is like a map of the old villages, each with its own story.

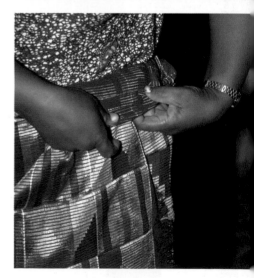

**Cecilia tucks her worgagba wrapper
securely around her waist.**

11

All Ewe cloth is "talking cloth."

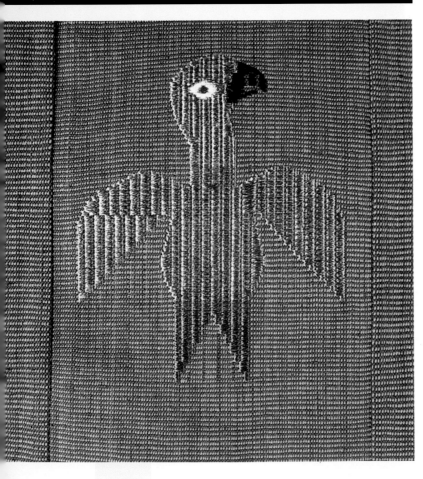

All Ewe cloth is "talking cloth." Children learn about their culture and history through the stories. "Talking Cloth" is Kweku's favorite storybook!

The elegant butterfly is hard-working and punctual.

Butterflies are not lazy. Kweku gets up as soon as he hears his father's footsteps in the early morning. Butterflies are already flying from flower to flower.

The parrot represents the power of nature.

If a person steals the red tail feather from a parrot, the feather will grow back! Nature is stronger than human beings.

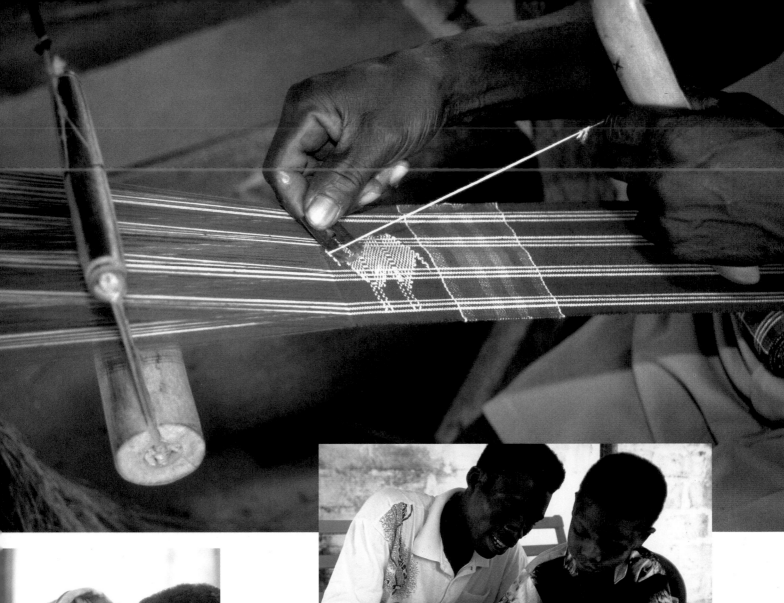

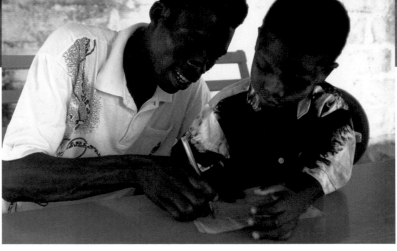

Kweku watches patiently as his father **inlays** the design of a goat, one thread at a time. Big brother Kwame shows Kweku how to write the word **"gbor"** (bor) Ewe for "goat", one letter at a time. Kweku tries to write "gbor" and then draws a picture of the family's sturdy little black gbor.

**Bright thread loops
hang to dry in the
sun-drenched courtyard.**

Each piece of Ewe strip weaving begins the same way...

The dyer puts clean white thread into a hot water bath. Dye powder is added. When the color is deep enough, the thread is pulled from the bath and hung in bright loops to dry in the sun.

Bobbo prefers to begin with thread that has already been dyed. He chooses the colors and quality he wants from the vast selection at the market in Agbozume. He likes to use cotton thread produced in Ghana, but buys thread imported from Egypt and India, too.

**The threads are dyed
outdoors in a big kettle
on a fire pit.**

Under his uncle's watchful eye,
Kweku winds a big bobbin.

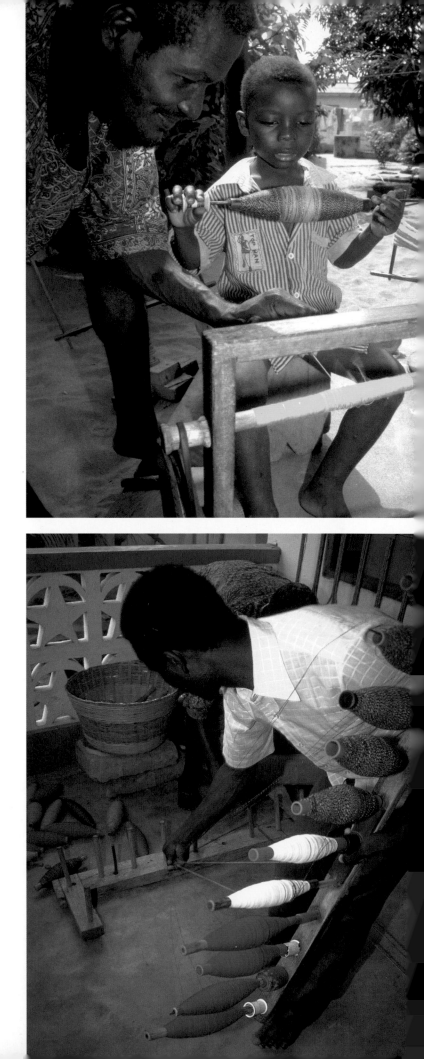

16

The thread is wound on hollow spools called **bobbins.** Each bobbin holds one color of thread. Twelve big bobbins are arranged on the rack that is used to measure enough thread to weave the new strip. Small bobbins, which hold less thread, are useful, too.

Each thread is 400 to 500 feet long! One strip of cloth can be longer than a football field from goal to goal!

These long threads are the warp threads.

There may be as many as 250 threads in the warp. All the threads must line up in a row.

Younger men prepare the bobbin racks. Then they walk up and down the long, covered walkway to lay out the warp threads.

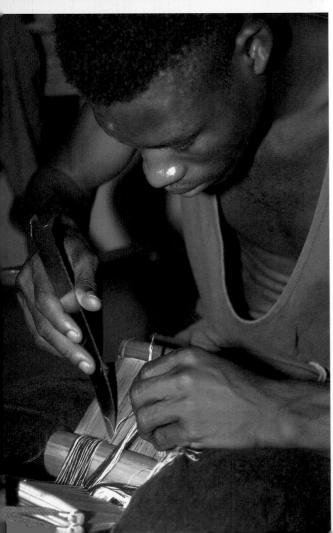

Kwame holds a string **heddle** between his knees. He feeds one end of each thread through a tiny space, like the eye of a needle. The heddles pull the long warp threads apart so the cross threads, the **weft**, can go through.

One heddle controls the even-numbered warp threads. Another heddle controls the odd-numbered warp threads. There are other ways to set up heddles. It depends on which design the weaver is making.

When the weaver creates an **inlaid design**, such as a goat, he pulls the warp threads apart with his fingers.

Each thread also has to go through the **beater**. The beater packs the threads to make a tight weave.

The free ends of all the long threads are carefully rolled up into a beautiful **crown**. The crowns ride on big, heavy drag-stones, placed far away from the weavers.

As the thread is needed, it is pulled toward the **loom**, unwinding as it goes. The stones make marks in the sand like those made by giant turtles.

The loom is the wooden frame that holds all the threads.

The loom is the weaver's partner. Without it, he cannot weave, so he treats his loom with honor and respect. Every day begins with prayers and songs of praise and gratitude.

The looms are narrow band **treadle** looms. Weavers work barefoot, using their toes to pull down on the cords that move the heddles. Their feet go up and down, one after the other.

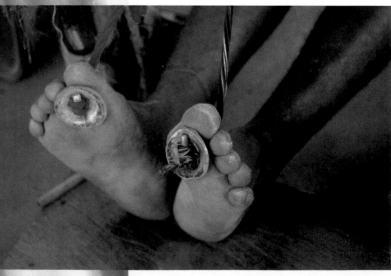

20

Each time the weaver presses down with his foot, the **warp sets** are pulled apart, creating a triangular space called a **shed.**

The **shuttle** holding the **weft** thread is passed through the shed from left to right. The beater is used to pack it in snugly.

When the weaver presses with his other foot, the warp pulls apart the other way. The weft is shuttled through from right to left, and is packed in again.

warp   shuttle   beater   shed   heddle

DANNY PECK

Bobbo concentrates totally when he weaves.

He works quickly and steadily. It takes three to four weeks to weave the long strip for a large wrapper, like Bobbo's green Sedavor with fences and animals.

The patterns he weaves are a time-honored part of his Ewe heritage, but a little bamboo measuring stick helps him make accurate changes in color and pattern.

Sometimes he sings to keep himself company. The song merges with the changing rhythm of his hands as he weaves the stories into the beautiful strip.

Under Kweku's watchful eye, Bobbo uses the shuttle.

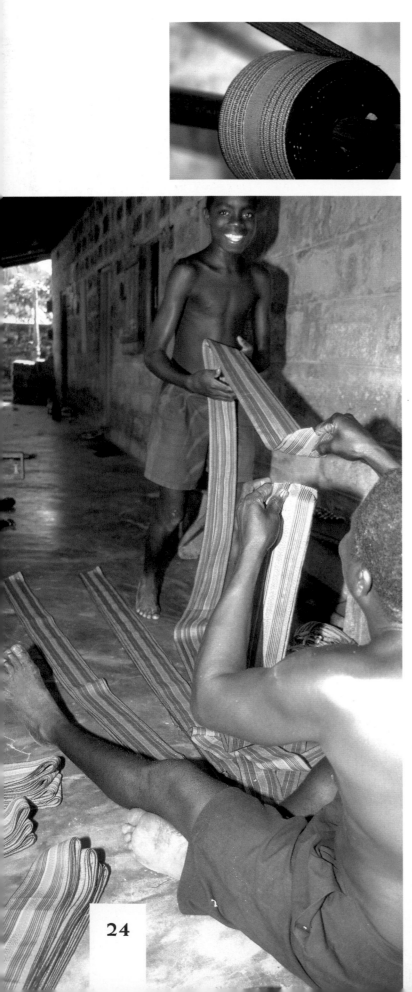

When all the thread in the crown is woven into cloth, the rolled up strip is taken off the loom, cut into even lengths, and stitched together.

The carefully woven strips have to line up to create the over all design of the wrapper. A man's wrapper is made up of 20 - 24 pieces. Women's wrappers are smaller.

Bobbo's old foot-powered treadle sewing machine does a good job, and is more reliable than his electric machine.

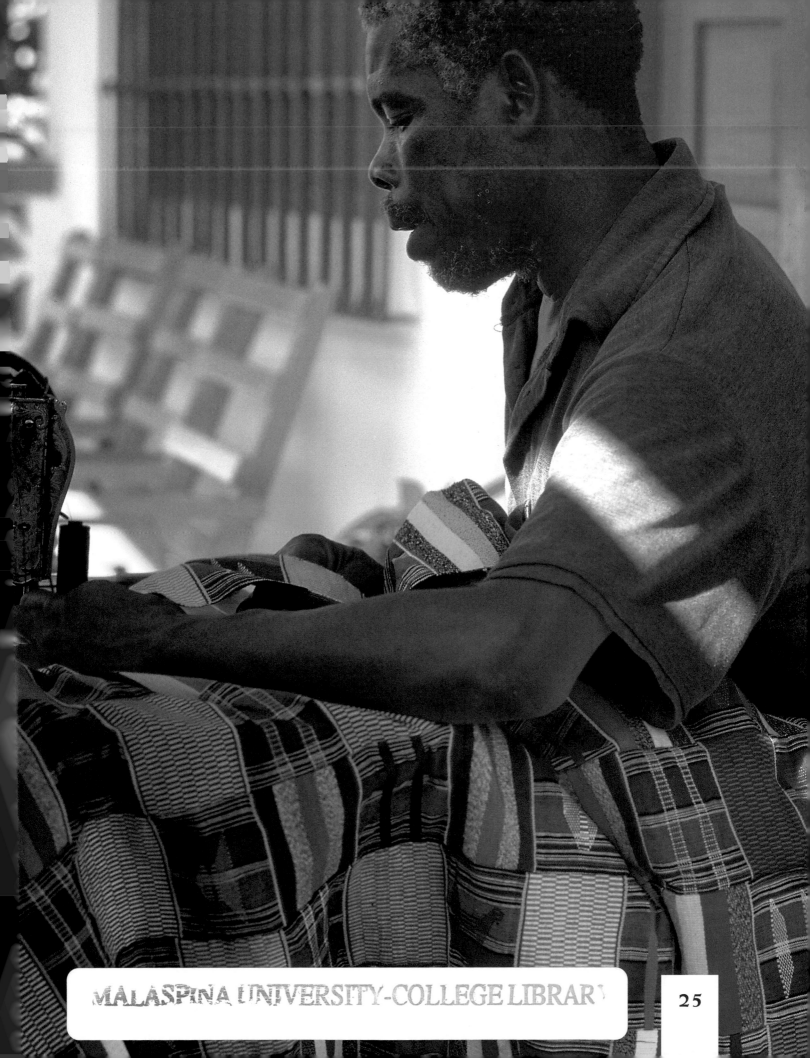

After the strips
are sewn together,
they do not look
like strips any more.
They become an
elegant wrapper
like this one.
Kwame wove it
himself and wore
it proudly at his
graduation.

All the while Bobbo was growing up, his country was undergoing great change. After more than 400 years of rule by European powers, Ghana gained its independence from England in 1957. Bobbo was thirteen years old. The people were proud and happy and there was great celebration the whole year long. Weavers made very special cloth for the occasion.

As a youngster, Bobbo expected he would be a weaver like his father. But as he grew older, he wanted to teach school. His math teacher, an American **Peace Corps** volunteer, had great respect and enthusiasm for Eve strip weaving. Bobbo was inspired by him to continue the family tradition.

Today, Bobbo is highly esteemed as a weaver and as a teacher. His magnificent strip weaving is sought after by people in Africa, Europe, Japan, and North America.

28

He has traveled to the Ivory Coast, Switzerland, the United States, and Canada to teach traditional West African strip weaving and to tell the stories of his people.

Bobbo's dream is to establish a weaving school in Denu where people from all over the world can come and watch and learn.

• • •

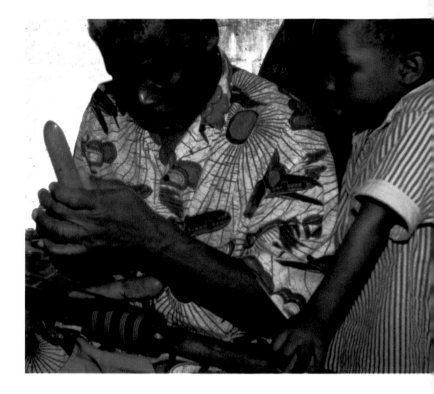

Kweku will soon join his father and brothers at the family looms. His new brother will wash threads, wind bobbins, and watch Bobbo weave threads into talking cloth.

When school begins, Kweku will already know a little English. He's been listening to the foreign guests who come to visit his father.

> Kweku is learning…
> not all weavers are men,
> not all men are fishermen
> or weavers, and weavers
> can be teachers, too!

The world is a loom that holds countless threads…

Suggested Reading for Children

Angelou, Maya. *Kofi and His Magic.*
New York: Clarkson N. Potter/Publishers, 1996.

Hintz, Martin. *Enchantment of the World: Ghana.*
Chicago: Childrens Press, 1994.

Suggested Reading for Adults

Adler, Peter & Nicholas Barnard. *African Majesty:*
The Textile Art of the Ashanti and Ewe.
London: Thames and Hudson, 1992.

Berry, LaVerle. *Ghana: A Country Study.*
Washington, DC: US Government Printing Office, 1995.

Gilfoy, Peggy Stoltz. *Patterns of Life: West African*
Strip-Weaving Traditions.
Washington, D.C.: Published for the National Museum
of African Art by the Smithsonian Institution Press, 1987.

Kent, Kate P. *West African Cloth.*
Denver, Colorado: Denver Museum of Natural History, 1971.

Lamb, Venice. *West African Weaving.*
London: Gerald Duckworth & Co. Ltd., 1975.

Supplemental Information

www.africanarts.com — a website dedicated to
bringing the arts and artisans of Africa online.

Vocabulary

beater ...... bamboo comb used to pack the newest weft thread into place

crown ...... roll of long threads waiting to be woven into the strip

dragstone . big stone that supports the crown

heddle ..... loops that hold the sets of warp threads so they can be
pulled apart

inlay .... (inlaid design) the picture pattern woven into Ewe cloth

loom .... wooden frame that holds all the threads

shed .... triangular space made when the warp threads are pulled apart

shuttle ..... tool that carries the thread back and forth to create the weft

treadle ..... foot-operated lever that moves the heddles on the loom
or the wheel and needle on a sewing machine

warp .... lengthwise threads in a weaving

weft .... cross threads in a weaving

NAMES.... Some, but not all, can be translated.

**Many West African children are named
after the day of the week on which they were born.**

DAY	BOY	GIRL	MEANING
SUNDAY	Kwesi	Akosua	under the sun
MONDAY	Kwadwo	Adwoa	peace
TUESDAY	Kwabena	Abena	fire
WEDNESDAY	Kwaku	Akua	fame
THURSDAY	Yao	Yaa	strength
FRIDAY	Kofi	Afua	growth
SATURDAY	Kwame	Ama	most ancient

Bobbo ..... Gilbert Ahiagble's nickname means "a big noise."

Acknowledgments

The authors wish to thank Sylvanus Anievor, Donnell Lewin, John Nash, and Toni Conklin for their help and encouragement in the development this book.

"Master Weaver from Ghana" was funded in part by the 1998 Margaret M. Conant Grant for Technical and Aesthetic Development in the Fiber Arts, awarded by Potomac Craftsmen Inc.

LOUISE MEYER is an educator who seeks to awaken interest in the social and economic value of native handicraft. She was working at the Museum of African Art in Washington, D.C. during **GILBERT BOBBO AHIAGBLE's** first U.S. visit in 1975. Later, while working on the Ivory Coast, she arranged an exhibition and workshop for Mr. Ahiagble which stimulated local weavers to further develop international and domestic markets. Ms. Meyer holds a B.A. and M.A. from the University of Maryland, and a diploma in African Studies from the Development Institute, Geneva, Switzerland. She resides in her native city, Washington, D.C. She can be reached on the Internet through www.africancrafts.com.

NESTOR HERNANDEZ was introduced to photography in high school through the Urban Journalism Workshop of the Washington, D.C. Public Schools. For fifteen years he was photographer-in-residence at the Capitol Children's Museum. As chief photographer for the Washington, D.C. Public Schools, he photographed Bobbo demonstrating weaving to school children. While visiting Bobbo in Denu, he learned to weave, and then took these photos. Nestor is of Afro-Cuban descent. Mr. Hernandez's work is exhibited in Cuba and the United States.

DANNY PECK photographed Bobbo at weaving workshops in Washington, D.C. Danny was instrumental in bringing this book to Open Hand Publishing Inc. Pictured with him is his daughter, Danielle. Now in fifth grade, Danielle advised Louise on the use of age-appropriate text in "Master Weaver." The Peck Studio in Rockville, Maryland, shared by Danny and his wife Gail, a graphic designer, serves primarily corporate clients.

32

OPEN HAND PUBLISHING, LLC
P. O. Box 20207
Greensboro, North Carolina 27420
336-292-8585
336-292-8588 FAX
E-mail: openhnd1@bellsouth.net
www.openhand.com

Cover, book design and production:
Deb Figen, ART & DESIGN SERVICE
Seattle, Washington
E-mail: artdesign@jps.net

**Library of Congress
Cataloging-in-Publication Data**

Ahiagble, Gilbert Bobbo, 1944-
    Master weaver from Ghana /
Gilbert Bobbo Ahiagble & Louise Meyer ;
photographs by Nestor Hernandez.
        p. cm.
    Includes biographical references (p. 30).
    Summary: A contemporary male weaver
from Ghana explains how his people maintain
the tradition of weaving, including an explanation
of the strip weaving of Kente cloth and its
importance in their Ewe culture.
    ISBN 0-940880-61-X (cloth)
        1. Male weavers--Ghana--Juvenile literature.
    2. Handloom industry--Ghana--Juvenile literature.
    [1. Hand weaving.   2. Ewe (African people)--
    Social life and customs.   3. Kente cloth.
    4. Ghana--Social life and customs.]
    I. Meyer, Louise, 1942-   .
    II. Hernandez, Nestor, ill.   III. Title.
    HD8039.T42G52 1998
    331.7'677'0282209667--dc21   98-26514
                                                        CIP
                                                        AC

Second Printing
Printed in Korea
05 04 03 02 01   6 5 4 3 2

GREEDY ZEBRA

LIBRARY OF CONGRESS CATALOG CARD NO. 83-83381

FIRST U.S. EDITION

BP

Published simultaneously in Canada
by Little, Brown & Company (Canada) Limited

PRINTED IN BELGIUM

GREEDY ZEBRA

by Mwenye Hadithi

Illustrated by Adrienne Kennaway

Little, Brown and Company

BOSTON   TORONTO

Long, long ago, all the animals in the world
were a dull, depressing color; no coats, no horns,
no spots, and no stripes. Just dull and dusty. Until...

One stormy day in the heart of the leafy forests of Africa there was a great rumbling in the earth, and all of a sudden a huge cave appeared in the ground. A few of the animals crept cautiously up to this new and wonderful sight, and when the bravest of them peered into the darkness he saw something glittering among the rocks.

The cave was full of furs and skins,
all glossy and new!
Stepping inside, he came across
horns and tails of countless
shapes and sizes,
and needles, and threads
of a thousand
different colors.
Trembling with excitement,
he rushed out to tell
the other animals
what he had seen.

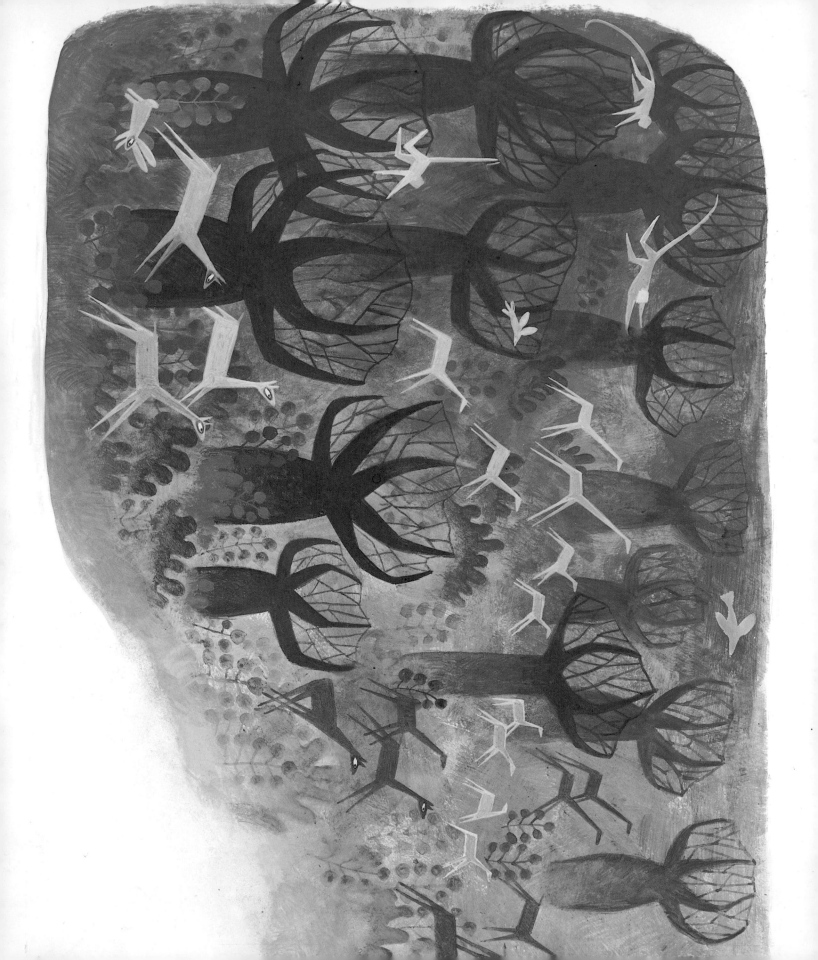

The news spread far and wide, and soon all the animals
were on their way to see the cave, running and jumping
and sliding and swinging,
and slithering through the trees.

All that is, except one — Greedy Zebra.

Greedy Zebra never ever stopped eating.

He certainly wasn't going to give up a single mouthful for a silly old cave of any sort.

"Lots of time to go visiting caves," mumbled Greedy Zebra, stuffing far too much grass into his bulging mouth.

"Plenty of time," he said.

Soon all the animals in the jungle were gathered at the mouth of the cave, waiting for Elephant to speak. Elephant was the one who knew everything. He coughed pompously, and addressed the gathering.

"It is time for you all to have coats," he said. "There are all kinds of materials here from which you may choose. You will be issued needles by Rabbit, but there is only one needle each, so take good care of it. Now you may go in — but no shoving and pushing, and keep in an orderly line!"

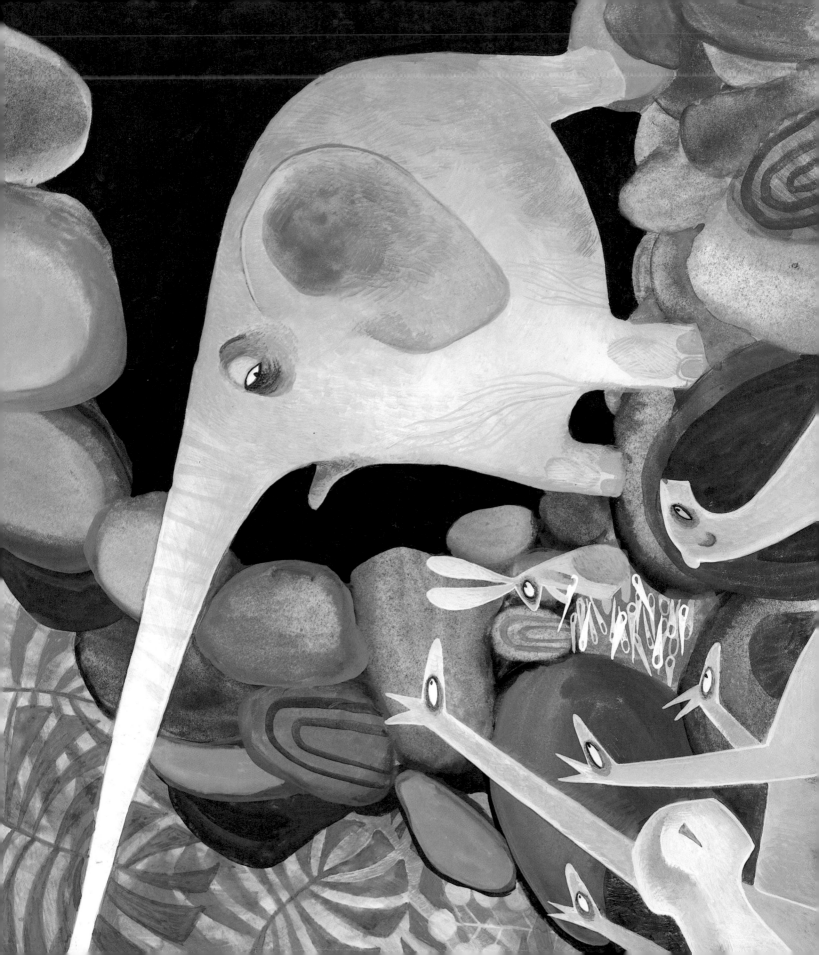

Meanwhile, Greedy Zebra was still eating. "Munch, munch," he went. "This particular grass is so delicious...." He stopped to gape at the beautiful thing in front of him. It couldn't be! But it was Sable the Antelope, and she was wearing the most glorious new coat. And horns! She was wearing horns!

When Greedy Zebra heard that the coat and horns came from the cave, he trotted off as fast as his fat little legs could carry him. But he couldn't resist a leaf here, or a succulent blade of grass there. Oh, and that patch was too good to pass by without one little bite!

From time to time he met another, and another,

and yet another,

of the wonderfully clothed animals. Stopping for a last bite not far from the cave, he watched Leopard finish her sewing. Leopard, as careful as usual, had sewn the most splendid fur coat with spots all over it. Greedy Zebra could not believe his eyes as he watched Leopard wriggle into a perfectly fitting fur.

"I shall have spots like that," he said to himself, and he hurried off, eager to reach the cave.

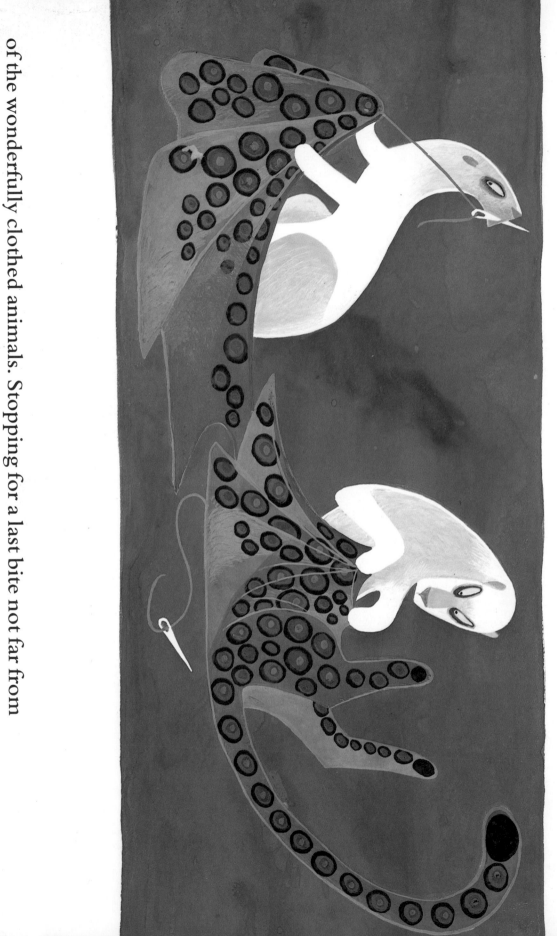

But it was a hot day, so he stopped for a cool drink at a stream, and there he came across a patch of the greenest grass he had ever seen.

"Delicious," he munched, smacking his chubby lips.

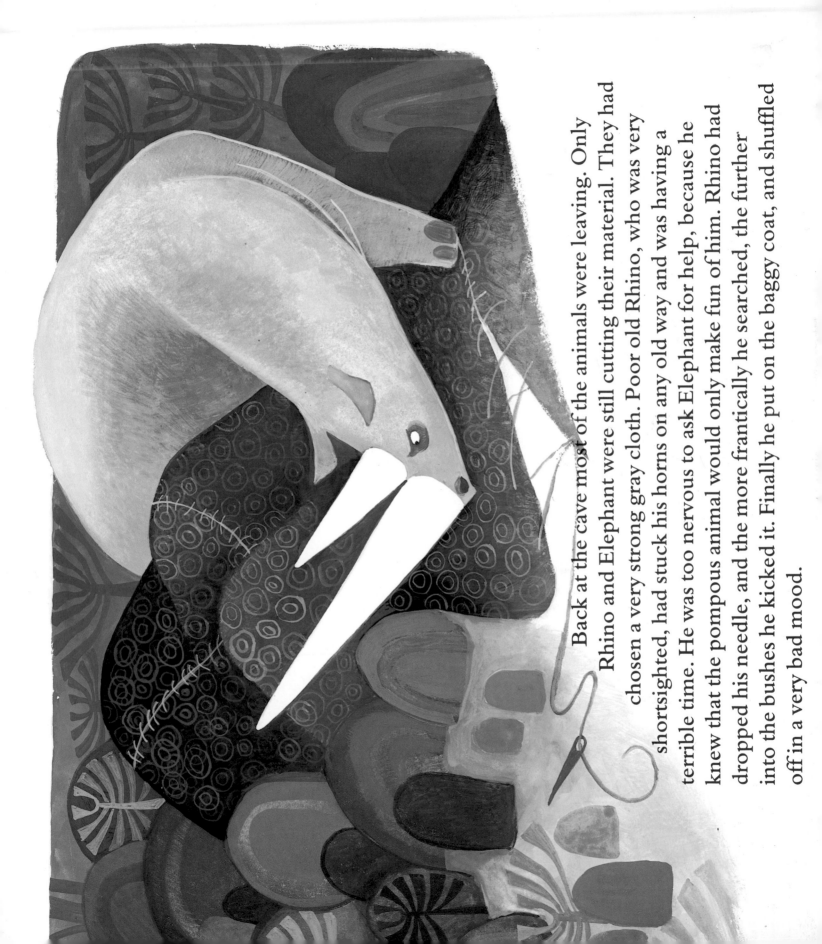

Back at the cave most of the animals were leaving. Only Rhino and Elephant were still cutting their material. They had chosen a very strong gray cloth. Poor old Rhino, who was very shortsighted, had stuck his horns on any old way and was having a terrible time. He was too nervous to ask Elephant for help, because he knew that the pompous animal would only make fun of him. Rhino had dropped his needle, and the more frantically he searched, the further into the bushes he kicked it. Finally he put on the baggy coat, and shuffled off in a very bad mood.

Just then Greedy Zebra trotted by,
with blades of grass bulging from his mouth.
"I'll have spots like Leopard," he was saying,
"and horns like Kudu, a mane like Lion, and
a tail like Cheetah. I shall be the
finest looking animal in the
forest!"

And at the risk of indigestion he gave a short gallop into the cave. Then he stopped, aghast.

There was nothing left! No horns, no fine cloth — nothing. Frantically he searched through the cave, but all he could find were a few strips of black material. Forlornly he cut them all to the same size and stitched them together.

"It looks very tight," he thought nervously to himself. Being such a very fat zebra, he had a terrible time squeezing into his coat. He pushed and grunted and oohed and aahed and — pop, he was inside it. But what a tight fit! It was nearly bursting at the seams around his fat tummy. He trotted down to the stream to take a quick bite of a leafy bush — and POP! his coat burst open.

POP!
POP!
POP!

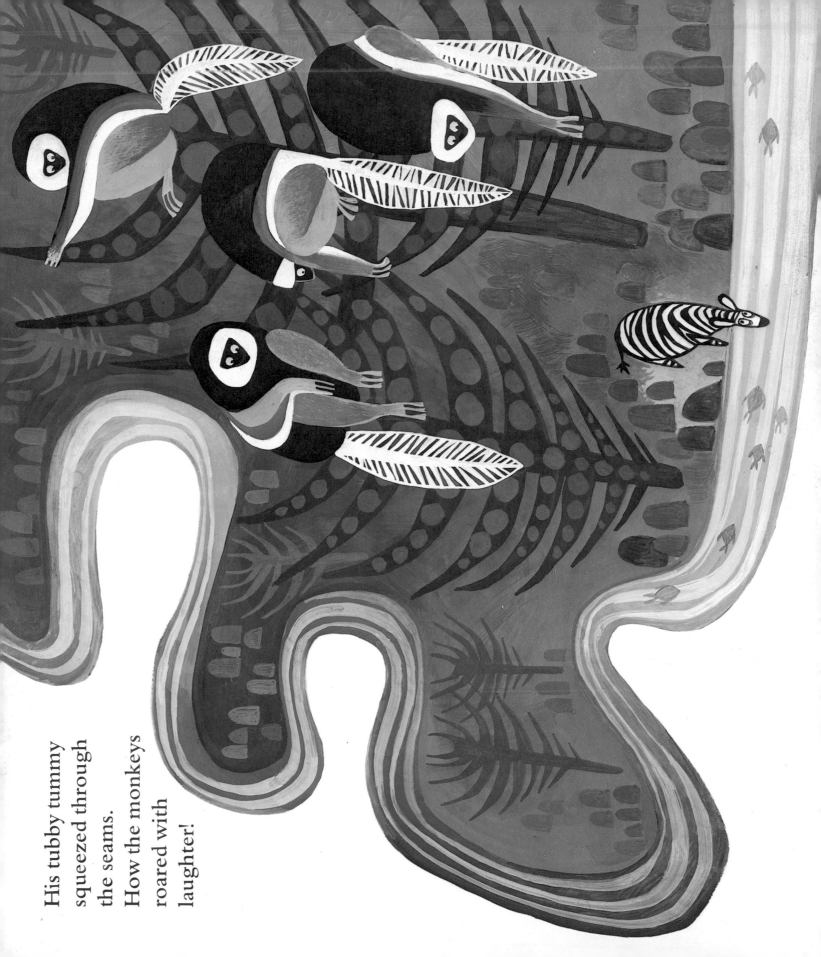

His tubby tummy
squeezed through
the seams.
How the monkeys
roared with
laughter!

To this day his chubby
stomach shines through
his coat because
he is so greedy.